Panoramic Journey Through

JOHANNESBURG

AND SURROUNDS

Panoramic Journey Through
JOHANNESBURG
AND SURROUNDS

First published in 2000 by Struik Publishers (Pty) Ltd
(a member of Struik New Holland Publishing (Pty) Ltd)

London • Cape Town • Sydney • Auckland

24 Nutford Place   14 Aquatic Drive
London W1H 6DQ   Frenchs Forest
United Kingdom   NSW 2086, Australia

80 McKenzie Street   218 Lake Road
Cape Town 8001   Northcote, Auckland
South Africa   New Zealand

10 9 8 7 6 5 4 3 2 1

ISBN 1 86872 469 7

DESIGNER Tracey Mackenzie
DESIGN MANAGER Janice Evans
EDITOR Lesley Hay-Whitton
MANAGING EDITOR Annlerie van Rooyen
PICTURE RESEARCHER Carmen Watts
FRENCH TRANSLATOR Jean-Paul Houssière
GERMAN TRANSLATOR Friedel Herrmann

Reproduction by Disc Express Cape (Pty) Ltd
Printed and bound by Times Offset (M) Sdn Bhd

ENDPAPERS *Bedfordview's Bruma Lake is a popular recreational centre.*
PAGE 1 *Sandton City, a shopper's paradise north of central Johannesburg.*
PAGES 2 AND 3 *Hartbeespoort Dam, one of the weekend retreats for residents of
Johannesburg and its surrounding areas.*
RIGHT *Johannesburg city centre.*

INTRODUCTION

Johannesburg is the capital of the province of Gauteng and the largest city in South Africa. Its Zulu name *eGoli* translates as 'place of gold', bearing testimony to the city's gold-mining history. Founded in the late 19th century after the discovery of gold on the Witwatersrand, Johannesburg has grown into the country's financial centre. For travellers, it is the starting point for excursions to the Magaliesberg hills, to the Pilanesberg National Park, to glittering Sun City and the Palace of the Lost City, and the world-famous Kruger National Park.

INTRODUCTION

Johannesburg, la capitale de la province de Gauteng, est la plus grande ville de l'Afrique du Sud. Son nom en zoulou, 'eGoli', signifie 'L'endroit où se trouve l'or', témoignant du passé minier de la cité. Fondée à la fin du 19ième siècle, suivant la découverte d'or dans le Witwatersrand, Johannesburg devint le siège financier du pays. C'est aussi le point de départ pour les excursions dans les collines du Magaliesberg, le Pilanesberg National Park, les lumières de Sun City et son 'Palace of the Lost City', ainsi que le Kruger National Park.

EINFÜHRUNG

Johannesburg ist die Hauptstadt der Region Gauteng und die größte Stadt in Südafrika. Der Zuluname 'eGoli' bedeutet 'Ort des Goldes' – ein Hinweis auf die geschichtliche Entwicklung durch die Goldminen. Johannesburg entstand im späten 19. Jahrhundert, nachdem auf dem Witwatersrand Gold entdeckt wurde und ist zum Finanzzentrum des Landes herangewachsen und Ausgangspunkt für Ausflüge zu den Magaliesberg-Hügeln, dem Pilanesberg Nationalpark, Sun City und Palace of Lost City und dem Kruger Nationalpark.

LEFT *Dramatic thunderstorms and lightning are a common feature of the Highveld summer.*

A GAUCHE *La foudre produit des effets dramatiques durant les orages d'été, une des caractéristiques du Highveld.*

LINKS *Gewitter mit Donner und Blitz kennzeichnen den Sommer auf dem Highveld.*

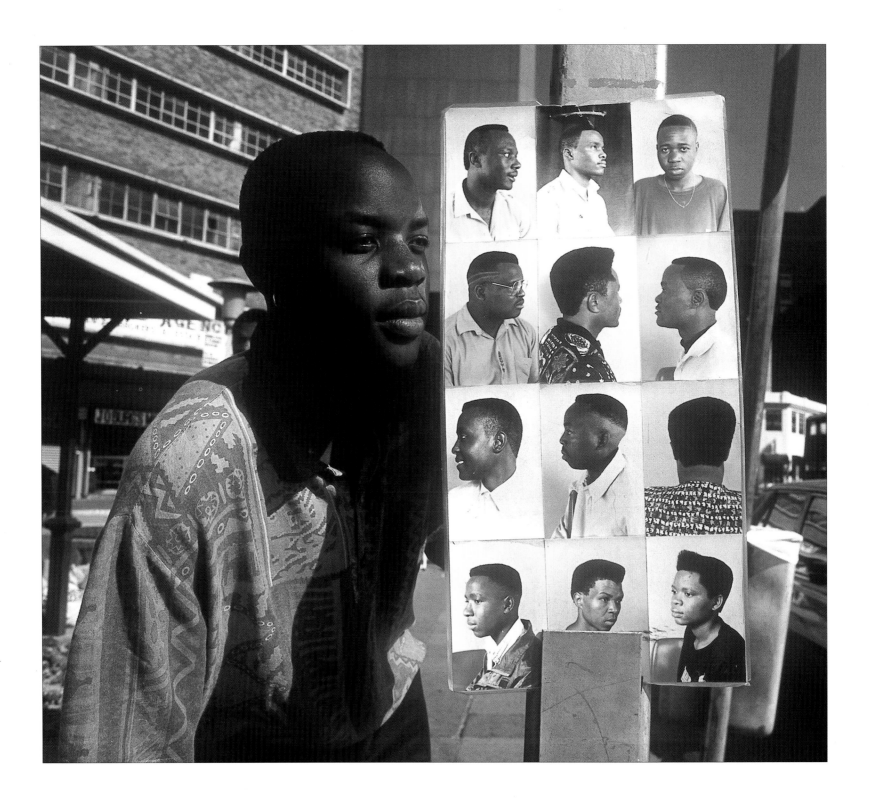

PAGES 8 AND 9 *Scenes from Johannesburg city centre: a street barber poses next to a board advertising the hairstyles on offer* (OPPOSITE), *a member of the Zionist church skilfully balances her purchases* (RIGHT) *and street hawkers display their wares* (BELOW).

PAGES 8 ET 9 *Dans le centre-ville de Johannesburg: un figaro pose à côté du panneau affichant ses diverses coiffures* (EN FACE). *Une fidèle de l'Église zioniste avec ses emplettes adroitement en équilibre sur la tête* (À DROITE). *Les colporteurs, étalant leurs marchandises* (CI-DESSOUS).

SEITEN 8 UND 9 *Szenen aus der Innenstadt von Johannesburg: ein Straßenfriseur posiert neben dem Schild mit seinem Frisurenangebot* (GEGENÜBER); *das Sternabzeichen kennzeichnet die Trägerin, die so geschickt ihre Einkäufe balanciert, als Glied der Zionistenkirche* (RECHTS); *Straßenverkäufer halten ihre Waren feil* (UNTEN).

LEFT *Dusk descends over central Johannesburg, bathing the buildings in a rosy light.*

A GAUCHE *Le crépuscule baigne les immeubles du centre de Johannesburg dans sa lumière rose.*

LINKS *Dämmerung senkt sich über das Stadtzentrum von Johannesburg und umhüllt die Gebäude mit einem rosa Schimmer.*

11

PAGES 12 AND 13 *Johannesburg is a city built on gold, the mine dumps a distinctive part of its landscape* (OPPOSITE). *Visitors are able to witness various aspects of gold-mining, such as gold-pouring* (RIGHT) *and mine dancers performing their traditional dances* (BELOW).

PAGES 12 ET 13 *Johannesburg est une ville dont les fondations reposent sur l'or, et les terrils de mines sont un spectacle familier* (EN FACE). *Les visiteurs pourront observer divers aspects de l'industrie aurifère, tels que la coulée de l'or en lingots et les danses traditionnelles des mineurs* (CI-DESSOUS).

SEITEN 12 UND 13 *Johannesburg ist eine Stadt, die auf Gold aufgebaut ist, und die Minenhalden gehören zur Landschaft* (GEGENÜBER). *Besucher können verschiedene Aspekte der Goldgewinnung beobachten, wie etwa das Gießen in Barren* (RECHTS) *und auch die traditionellen Tänze der Minenarbeiter* (UNTEN).

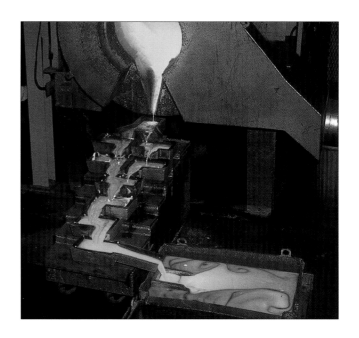

LEFT *The Market Theatre situated in Johannesburg's Newtown area is the venue for many of the city's performing arts and music happenings.*

A GAUCHE *Le Market Theatre dans le quartier de Newtown, à Johannesburg, où se donnent de nombreuses représentations et concerts.*

LINKS *Das Market Theater im Johannesburger Stadtbezirk Newtown bietet Aufführungen und musikalische Darbietungen.*

RIGHT AND BELOW *Outside the Market Theatre a lively fleamarket operates during the day .*

A DROITE ET CI-DESSOUS *Un marché aux puces animé est ouvert durant la journée en face du Market Theatre.*

RECHTS UND UNTEN *Vor dem Market Theater findet tagsüber ein lebhafter Flohmarkt statt.*

OPPOSITE *Ndebele dolls and beadwork on sale at the informal fleamarket outside the Market Theatre.*
EN FACE *A l'extérieur du Market Theatre. Poupées et ouvrages de perles Ndebele en vente aux touristes.*
GEGNÜBER *Eine Auswahl von Perlenarbeiten und Puppen der Ndebele.*

ABOVE *Zulu dancers and live music entertain passers-by at the Market Theatre fleamarket.*
CI-DESSUS *Des Zouloues dansent pour les flâneurs, au marché aux puces du Market Theatre.*
OBEN *Zulutänzer tragen zur Unterhaltung auf dem Flohmarkt bei.*

ABOVE *In the Adler Museum of the History of Medicine a turn-of-the-century pharmacy has been painstakingly recreated.*
CI-DESSUS *La reproduction d'une pharmacie du début du siècle à l'Adler Museum of the History of Medicine.*
OBEN *Im Adlermuseum für Medizingeschichte hat man sorgfältig eine Apotheke der Jahrhundertwende aufgebaut.*

ABOVE *MuseumAfrica, launched in 1994, records the history of the subcontinent through various exhibits including squatter shacks.*
CI-DESSUS *Au MuseumAfrica, fondé en 1994, les expositions des archives et comptes – rendus racontent l'histoire du sous-continent.*
OBEN *MuseumAfrica, 1994 eröffnet, präsentiert die Geschichte des Subkontinents – wie Umsiedlungen der Elendsviertel – in Ausstellungen.*

OPPOSITE *Customers buying* muti *(traditional medicine) in an African medicine shop in the centre of Johannesburg.*
EN FACE *Clients achetant du* muti, *(remèdes traditionnels) dans une herboristerie.*
GEGENÜBER *Kunden in einem afrikanischen Heilmittelgeschäft kaufen* Muti *(traditionelle Heilerzeugnisse).*

PAGES 20 AND 21 *Gold Reef City is a reconstructed mining town* (BELOW). *Children who fit under the statue's hand* (OPPOSITE) *have free entrance.*
PAGES 20 ET 21 *Gold Reef City* (CI-DESSOUS) *reproduction d'une ville minière. Les enfants qui passent sous la main* (EN FACE) *entrent gratuitement.*
SEITEN 20 UND 21 *Gold Reef City ist ein rekonstruierter Minenort* (UNTEN). *Wer unter der Hand stehen kann* (GEGENÜBER), *hat freien Zugang.*

FOLLOWING PAGES *Zulu dancers in front of Gold Reef City Hotel; in the background a horse-drawn carriage waits to transport people.*
PAGES SUIVANTES *Des danseuses Zouloues en face du Gold Reef City Hotel; au fond, une charrette à cheval pour le transport des visiteurs.*
UMSEITIG *Zulutänzerinnen vor dem Gold Reef City Hotel; im Hintergrund warten Pferdekutschen auf Fahrgäste.*

21

ABOVE *The steam train that carries visitors around Gold Reef City.*

CI-DESSUS *Le train à vapeur pour les visiteurs de Gold Reef City.*

OBEN *Der Dampfzug, der Besucher in Gold Reef City herumfährt.*

OPPOSITE *'Wild Water Run', one of the entertainments at Gold Reef City.*

EN FACE *'Wild Water Run', une des attractions de Gold Reef City.*

GEGENÜBER *'Wild Water Run', eine der Belustigungen in Gold Reef City.*

PAGES 26 AND 27 *Among the attractions of Santarama Miniland* (LEFT) *is a replica of the* Drommedaris (ABOVE), *the ship which brought white settlers to the Cape in the 17th century.*
PAGES 26 ET 27 *Parmi les attractions de Santarama Miniland* (À GAUCHE) *se trouve une reproduction du* Drommedaris (CI-DESSUS), *le navire qui, au 17ième siècle, apporta les colons blancs au Cap.*
SEITEN 26 UND 27 *Eine große Attraktion im Santarama Miniland* (LINKS) *ist die Nachbildung der* Drommedaris (OBEN), *eines der Schiffe, die im 17. Jahrhundert die ersten weißen Siedler aus Europa ans Kap brachten.*

OPPOSITE *Fisherman's Village, set on Bedfordview's Bruma Lake, is a delightful place to eat and shop, or go boating and windsurfing.*
EN FACE *Fisherman's Village, situé sur les bords de Bruma Lake, à Bedfordview, est un endroit charmant pour les courses, manger au restaurant, ou faire des sports aquatiques.*
GEGENÜBER *Fisherman's Village, am Bruma-See in Bedfordview, ist ein charmanter Ort zum Einkaufen, Speisen, Boot fahren und Windsegeln.*

BELOW LEFT AND RIGHT *A South American musician* (LEFT) *and the Mardi Gras* (RIGHT) *at the Bruma Lake fleamarket.*
CI-DESSOUS À GAUCHE ET À DROITE *Un musicien sud-américain* (À GAUCHE) *et un carnaval* (À DROITE) *au marché aux puces de Bruma Lake .*
UNTEN LINKS UND RECHTS *Ein südamerikanischer Musikant* (LINKS) *und der Karneval* (RECHTS) *auf dem Flohmarkt am Bruma-See.*

ABOVE *Street musicians provide entertainment for shoppers browsing at the Bruma Lake fleamarket.*
CI-DESSUS *Des musiciens ambulants divertissent les flâneurs au marché aux puces de Bruma Lake.*
OBEN *Während die Käufer auf dem Flohmarkt am Bruma-See herumbummeln, sorgen Straßenmusikanten für Unterhaltung.*

OPPOSITE *Zoo Lake is one of Johannesburg's most popular outdoor areas, where leisurely hours can be spent picnicking or boating.*
EN FACE *Le Zoo Lake est un des endroits de plein air des plus populaires de Johannesburg. On y passe le temps à pique-niquer ou faire du canotage.*
GEGENÜBER *Zoo Lake ist eine der beliebtesten Erholungsstätten in Johannesburg für geruhsame Stunden beim Bootfahren oder Picknick.*

PAGES 32 AND 33 *North-west of central Johannesburg, Emmarentia Dam is another*
of the city's more scenic recreational options, where boaters take to the waters in canoes
(ABOVE) or yachts (RIGHT).

PAGES 32 ET 33 *Emmarentia Dam, au nord ouest de Johannesburg, est un des autres*
endroits de loisir où se retrouvent les amateurs de canoë (CI-DESSUS) et de voile (À DROITE).

SEITEN 32 UND 33 *Nordwestlich vom Johannesburger Stadtkern gelegen, bietet der Emmarentia*
Dam eine weitere Freizeitoption, wo Kanus (OBEN) und Jachten (RECHTS) den See bevölkern.

PREVIOUS PAGES *Sandton, one of the affluent satellite towns just
north of Johannesburg, is a shopper's mecca.*
PAGES PRÉCÉDENTES *Sandton, une riche agglomération au nord
de Johannesburg, possède de nombreux magasins de grand luxe.*
VORIGE SEITEN *Sandton, eine der wohlhabenden Satellitenstädte
im Norden von Johannesburg, ist ein Mekka für Einkaufslustige. Das
Warenangebot hier hat absolut Weltklasse.*

PAGES 36 AND 37 *Café Renoir, one of Sandton City's many restaurants*
(ABOVE). *Sandton Square, a business, retail and arts complex* (OPPOSITE).
PAGES 36 ET 37 *Le Café Renoir, un des nombreux restaurants de Sandton
City* (CI-DESSUS). *Sandton Square, un centre commercial et artistique* (EN FACE).
SEITEN 36 UND 37 *Café Renoir, eines der vielen Restaurants in Sandton
City* (OBEN). *Sandton Square, ein Komplex für Unternehmen, Geschäfte
und Kunsthandlungen* (GEGENÜBER).

PAGES 38 AND 39 *Village Walk is one of Sandton's airy and attractive shopping centres* (ABOVE). *Outside the centre, street vendors sell crafts from many parts of Africa* (RIGHT).
PAGES 38 ET 39 *'Village Walk' est un autre charmant centre commercial de Sandton* (CI-DESSUS), *où l'on trouve des objets artisanaux provenant de nombreux endroits d'Afrique* (À DROITE).
SEITEN 38 UND 39 *Village Walk ist eines der ansprechenden, hellen Einkaufszentren in Sandton* (OBEN), *wo Straßenverkäufer Handgearbeitetes aus ganz Afrika anbieten* (RECHTS).

PAGES 40 AND 41 *The Randburg Waterfront, a popular shopping and entertainment venue.*

PAGES 40 ET 41 *Le 'Randburg Waterfront', un centre commercial et de loisirs populaire.*

SEITEN 40 UND 41 *Die Randburg Waterfront, ein schöner Einkaufs- und Unterhaltungskomplex.*

BELOW One of the Randburg Waterfront's numerous eateries.
CI-DESSOUS Un des nombreux restaurants au Randburg Waterfront.
UNTEN Eines der vielen Speiselokale in der Randburg Waterfront.

RIGHT The Randburg Waterfront's 'Fountains of Light' provide spectacular displays in the evenings. This 50-m-long musical fountain is said to be the largest of its kind in the world.
A DROITE Les 'Fountains of Light' au Randburg Waterfront. Cette fontaine musicale de 50m, qui est illuminée en soirée, est une des plus longues du monde dans le genre.
RECHTS Abends erstrahlt die 'Fountains of Light' an der Randburg Waterfront. Diese 50m hohe, musikalisch untermalte Lichtfontäne soll die größte ihrer Art in der Welt sein.

PAGES 44 AND 45 *The Witwatersrand National Botanical Garden, Roodepoort, protects the Rand's indigenous vegetation. The garden boasts many interesting features, such as Witpoortjie Waterfall* (LEFT), *which plunges into a ravine, and a sundial* (ABOVE).

PAGES 44 ET 45 *Le 'Witwatersrand National Botanical Garden' à Roodepoort est un conservatoire pour la flore indigène du Rand. La cascade 'Witpoortjie Waterfall'* (À GAUCHE) *se précipite dans un ravin, et un cadran solaire embellit le décor* (CI-DESSUS).

SEITEN 44 UND 45 *Der Nationale Botanische Garten Witwatersrand in Roodepoort ist der einheimischen Vegetation gewidmet. Der Witpoortjie Wasserfall* (LINKS) *ergießt sich in eine Schlucht. Interessant ist auch die Sonnenuhr* (OBEN).

OPPOSITE *West of Johannesburg, Florida Lake, where waterbirds breed.*
EN FACE *Florida Lake, où se reproduisent les oiseaux aquatiques.*
GEGENÜBER *Der Florida-See dient als Brutstätte für Wasservögel.*

BELOW LEFT AND RIGHT *Heia Safari Ranch's traditional Zulu village.*
CI-DESSOUS *Traditionnel village Zoulou à Heia Safari Ranch.*
UNTEN LINKS UND RECHTS *Ein Zuludorf auf der Heia Safari Ranch.*

FOLLOWING PAGES *Pretoria, lying some 56 km from Johannesburg, is South Africa's administrative capital. The Union Buildings (floodlit in the background) were designed by Herbert Baker.*
PAGES SUIVANTES *Pretoria, à quelque 56 km de Johannesburg; au fond, 'Union Buildings' où eut lieu la cérémonie d'investiture de Mandela.*
UMSEITIG *In Pretoria, etwa 56km von Johannesburg entfernt, stehen die 'Union Buildings', wo Mandela als President vereidigt wurde.*

OPPOSITE *Pretoria's City Hall is situated on Pretorius Plain, flanked
by the ubiquitous purple jacaranda trees.*

EN FACE *L'Hôtel de Ville de Pretoria, sur Pretorius Plain, bordée par
les omniprésents jacarandas.*

GEGENÜBER *Das Rathaus von Pretoria steht auf dem Pretorius-Platz,
der von lila blühenden Jakarandabäumen umringt ist.*

ABOVE *Anton van Wouw's statue of President Paul Kruger watches
over Church Square, Pretoria's hub.*

CI-DESSUS *Sculpté par Anton van Wouw, Paul Kruger observe le va-et-
vient à Church Square, au coeur de Pretoria.*

OBEN *Anton van Wouws Standbild von President Paul Kruger blickt
auf Pretorias Church Square (Kirchenplatz), dem Mittelpunkt der Stadt.*

BELOW   *The imposing Voortrekker Monument, 3 km south of central Pretoria, commemorates the Great Trek of the 1830s and 1840s.*
CI-DESSOUS   *L'imposant Voortrekker Monument, à 3km au sud de Pretoria, fut érigé pour marquer le 'Great Trek' des années 1830 et '40.*
UNTEN   *Das imposante Voortrekkerdenkmal, 3km südlich von Pretoria, erinnert an den Großen Trek, der sich in den Jahren um 1840 vollzog.*

OPPOSITE   *Melrose House, where the Treaty of Vereeniging, which ended the Second Anglo-Boer War, was signed in May 1902.*
EN FACE   *Melrose House, où fut ratifié l'historique Treaty of Vereeniging, en mai 1902.*
GEGENÜBER   *Melrose House, wo im Mai 1902 der Friedensvertrag von Vereeniging, der den Burenkrieg beendete, unterzeichnet wurde.*

OPPOSITE *A monument to Louis Botha, South Africa's first prime minister.*

EN FACE *La statue de Louis Botha à l''Union Buildings'.*

GEGENÜBER *Standbild von Louis Botha vor den 'Union Buildings'.*

ABOVE *The Union Buildings are set in attractive gardens.*

CI-DESSUS *'L'Union Buildings' est l'oeuvre d'Herbert Baker.*

OBEN *Die 'Union Buildings' wurden von Herbert Baker entworfen.*

PAGES 56 AND 57 *The Ndebele people, seen here at Botshabelo Cultural Village near Middelburg, east of Johannesburg, are renowned for their distinctive dress and brightly coloured geometric murals.*

PAGES 56 ET 57 *Les Ndebele, ici à Botshabelo, sont renommés pour leur costume caractéristique et leurs fresques aux formes géométriques multicolores.*

SEITEN 56 UND 57 *Die Ndebele – hier in Botshabelo – sind bekannt für ihre außergewöhnliche Tracht und ihre farbenfreudigen Wandmalereien in geometrischen Motiven.*

PAGES 58 AND 59 *An Ndebele homestead, with characteristic thatched roofs and colourfully painted walls* (LEFT). *Even the interiors of some of the houses are decorated* (BELOW).
PAGES 58 ET 59 *Des habitations Ndebele au toit de chaume caractéristique et leurs murs aux couleurs vives* (À GAUCHE). *Même l'intérieur des maisons est pareillement décoré* (CI-DESSOUS).
SEITEN 58 UND 59 *Eine Ndebele Heimstätte: das Reetdach und die bunt bemalten Wände sind charakteristisch* (LINKS). *Auch die Innenwände der Häuser sind bemalt* (UNTEN).

ABOVE *Warm Baths is a favourite holiday resort north of Pretoria in Northern Province.*

CI-DESSUS *Warm Baths, un centre de villégiature au nord de Prétoria, dans Northern Province.*

OBEN *Warm Baths, ein Ferienort nördlich von Pretoria, liegt in der angrenzenden Nordprovinz.*

ABOVE   *Warm Baths' wave pool is popular with the young and young-at-heart.*

CI-DESSUS   *La piscine de Warm Baths est populaire avec les jeunes et les moins jeunes.*

OBEN   *Das Wellenbad in Warm Baths ist beliebt bei Jung und Alt.*

PAGES 62 AND 63 *The Magaliesberg range stretches 120 km to the west of Pretoria. A hot-air balloon* (LEFT) *and steam train* (ABOVE) *are among the ways to explore this beautiful region.*
PAGES 62 ET 63 *La chaîne du Magaliesberg s'étend sur 120km, à l'ouest de Prétoria. On peut explorer cette belle région en montgolfière* (À GAUCHE) *ou en train à vapeur* (CI-DESSUS).
SEITEN 62 UND 63 *Die Magaliesbergkette erstreckt sich westlich von Pretoria über 120km. Man kann dieses schöne Gebiet auch im Heißluftballon* (LINKS) *und mit dem Dampfzug* (OBEN) *erkunden.*

ABOVE *Retief Kloof, one of the many attractions of the Magaliesberg.*

CI-DESSUS *Retief Kloof, une des nombreuses attractions touristiques du Magaliesberg.*

OBEN *Retief Kloof ist eine der vielen Sehenswürdigkeiten in den Magaliesbergen.*

ABOVE *Nature lovers can follow a variety of hiking trails in the Magaliesberg, ranging in length from one hour to four days.*

CI-DESSUS *Les amateurs de randonnées trouveront dans Le Magaliesberg un choix de nombreux itinéraires.*

OBEN *Für Naturfreunde gibt es Wanderwege in den Magaliesbergen, für die man von einer Stunde bis zu vier Tagen benötigt.*

PAGES 66 AND 67 *Speedboats and yachts on Hartbeespoort Dam. The dam is within easy reach of Johannesburg and Pretoria and is set in scenic surroundings at the foot of the Magaliesberg range.*

PAGES 66 ET 67 *Hors bords et voiliers à Hartbeespoort Dam, à moins d'une heure de route de Johannesburg et Pretoria. Le lac est situé dans un décor enchanteur, au pied de la chaîne du Magaliesberg.*

SEITEN 66 UND 67 *Jachten und Schnellboote auf dem Hartbeespoort Dam, der nur eine Autostunde von Johannesburg und Pretoria in der malerischen Umgebung am Fuße der Magaliesberge liegt.*

PAGES 68 AND 69 *Hartbeespoort Dam is a popular retreat for city dwellers, providing them with ample recreational opportunities.*

PAGES 68 ET 69 *Hartbeespoort Dam est un endroit de prédilection pour les sports aquatiques. On peut y passer de nombreuses heures à pêcher et à la navigation de plaisance.*

SEITEN 68 UND 69 *Wassersportenthusiasten können sich auf dem Hartbeespoort Dam endlos mit Bootsfahrten und Angeln vergnügen.*

OPPOSITE *A game-viewing hide in the Pilanesberg National Park.*

EN FACE *Une cachette d'observation au Pilanesberg National Park.*

GEGENÜBER *Wildbeobachtungsversteck im Pilanesberg Nationalpark.*

BELOW *Elephant are among the game to be seen in the Pilanesberg.*

CI-DESSOUS *Les visiteurs à Pilanesberg y trouveront des éléphants.*

UNTEN *Zu den Wildarten im Pilanesberg zählen auch Elefanten.*

ABOVE   *Zebra at a waterhole in the Pilanesberg National Park, adjacent to Sun City.*

CI-DESSUS   *Zèbres à un point d'eau, au Pilanesberg National Park.*

OBEN   *Zebras an der Wasserstelle im Pilanesberg Nationalpark.*

ABOVE *Pilanesberg has various comfortable camps, among them Bakubung Lodge.*

CI-DESSUS *Bakubung Lodge, un des nombreux camps dans le Pilanesberg.*

OBEN *Bakubung Lodge ist eines der komfortablen Rastlager im Pilanesberg Wildpark.*

PAGES 74 AND 75 *The Palace of the Lost City is a glittering pleasure park in North-West province, its hotel* (OPPOSITE) *offering luxurious accommodation. The entrance to the Palace is graced by a bronze sculpture depicting a cheetah hunt* (BELOW), *while Crystal Court is opulent and airy* (RIGHT).

PAGES 74 ET 75 *Le 'Palace of the Lost City' est un flamboyant centre de villégiature dans la province de North West. Son hôtel de grand luxe* (EN FACE) *a une entrée ornée d'un bronze représentant un guépard à l'affût* (CI-DESSOUS). *Le 'Crystal Court' est spacieux et opulent* (À DROITE).

SEITEN 74 UND 75 *Palace of the Lost City ist ein glitzernder Vergnügungskomplex in der Nordwestprovinz. Das Hotel* (GEGENÜBER) *bietet luxuriöse Unterkunft. Den Eingang ziert eine Bronzeskulptur, die einen Geparden beim Riß darstellt* (UNTEN). *Crystal Court* (RECHTS) *ist großzügig angelegt und fürstlich ausgestattet.*

PAGES 76 AND 77 *The myriad attractions of the Sun City/Lost City complex include a simulated earthquake* (RIGHT), *the Bridge of Time* (BOTTOM) *and the Palace's Wave Pool* (OPPOSITE).

PAGES 76 ET 77 *Parmi les innombrables attractions du complexe Sun City/Lost City, on trouvera un tremblement de terre artificiel* (À DROITE), *le 'Bridge of Time'* (EN BAS) *et une piscine à vagues* (EN FACE).

SEITEN 76 UND 77 *Zu den vielfältigen Attraktionen von SunCity/Lost City zählen ein simuliertes Erdbeben* (RECHTS), *die 'Bridge of Time' – Brücke der Zeit –* (UNTEN) *und das Wellenbad im Palace* (GEGENÜBER).

FOLLOWING PAGES *The Valley of the Waves is a popular and fun place to cool down on a hot summer's day in the bushveld.*

PAGES SUIVANTES *La 'Valley of the Waves' est populaire pour se rafraîchir en brousse de la chaleur estivale.*

UMSEITIG *Valley of the Waves (Tal der Wellen) ist ein beliebter Ort, wo es Spaß macht, sich an einem heißen Sommertag in der Baumsavanne abzukühlen.*

PAGES 80 AND 81 *At Sun City the Cascades Hotel* (OPPOSITE) *offers upmarket accommodation, while the Entertainment Centre provides round-the-clock amusement* (RIGHT). *Visitors can also see crocodiles at the Kwena Gardens* (BELOW).

PAGES 81 ET 81 *Le Cascades Hotel* (EN FACE) *de Sun City, est un hôtel haut de gamme; L'Entertainment Centre' est ouvert en permanence* (À DROITE). *Les visiteurs verront aussi des crocodiles dans les 'Kwena Gardens'* (CI-DESSOUS).

SEITEN 80 UND 81 *Das Cascade's Hotel in Sun City* (GEGENÜBER) *bietet gehobene Unterkunftsmöglichkeiten und im Entertainment Centre gibt es Abwechslung rund um die Uhr* (RECHTS). *In den Kwena Gardens können Besucher auch Krokodile sehen* (UNTEN).

PREVIOUS PAGES *The Kruger National Park's Olifants Camp is on the eastern side of the park.*

PAGES PRÉCÉDENTES *Olifants Camp, est situé dans la partie orientale du Kruger Park.*

VORIGE SEITE *Das Olifant's Camp Rastlager liegt auf der Ostseite des Kruger Nationalparks.*

PAGES 84 AND 85 *The Kruger boasts the 'Big Five', among them lion* (LEFT) *and elephant* (BELOW).

PAGES 84 ET 85 *Le Kruger Park est l'habitat du lion* (À GAUCHE) *et l'éléphant* (CI-DESSOUS).

SEITEN 84 UND 85 *Hier gibt es die 'Großen Fünf' – darunter Löwen* (LINKS) *und Elefanten* (UNTEN).

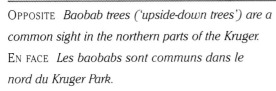

OPPOSITE *Baobab trees ('upside-down trees') are a common sight in the northern parts of the Kruger.*
EN FACE *Les baobabs sont communs dans le nord du Kruger Park.*
GEGENÜBER *Boabab (Affenbrotbäume) sind im nördlichen Teil des Kruger Nationalparks weitverbreitet.*

PAGE 87 *Among the Kruger's abundant birdlife are the lilac-breasted roller (TOP LEFT) and the bateleur (ABOVE).*
PAGE 87 *Parmi les nombreux habitants ailés du Kruger Park, on trouve le rollier à longs brins (CI-DESSUS À GAUCHE) et le bateleur des savanes (CI-DESSUS À DROITE).*
SEITE 87 *Die reiche Vogelwelt im Kruger Nationalpark beheimatet auch die Gabelracke (OBEN LINKS) und den Gaukler (OBEN RECHTS).*

PAGES 88 AND 89 *At Bateleur Camp visitors to the Kruger watch animals from the safety of a hide* (ABOVE). *The leopard, one of the Big Five, can be seen in the park* (LEFT). *Dwarfed by a giraffe, impala drink from a waterhole* (OPPOSITE).

PAGES 88 ET 89 *A 'Bateleur Camp', au Kruger Park, les visiteurs, dissimulés dans une cachette, pourront observer les bêtes en toute sécurité* (CI-DESSUS). *Le Kruger Park est aussi l'habitat de nombreux léopards* (À GAUCHE). *Diminués par la taille d'une girafe, les impalas se désaltèrent au point d'eau* (EN FACE).

SEITEN 88 UND 89 *Im Bateleur Camp Rastlager beobachten Besucher die Tiere im Schutz eines Verstecks* (OBEN). *Der Leopard, der auch zu den 'Großen Fünf' zählt, ist im Kruger Nationalpark ebenfalls anzutreffen* (LINKS). *Neben der Giraffe wirkt die Schwarzfersenantilope (Impala) sehr klein* (GEGENÜBER).

PAGES 90 AND 91 *Game-viewing is not the only option in the Kruger. Among the other attractions of the park are the Late Iron Age site at the Masorini Open-Air Museum* (OPPOSITE) *and tablets paying tribute to Paul Kruger, after whom the park is named* (RIGHT). *The rest camps have attractive restaurants, such as this one at Letaba* (BOTTOM).

PAGES 90 ET 91 *Le Kruger Park offre d'autres attractions touristiques outre les animaux. Au musée en plein air de Masorini, on pourra explorer un site archéologique datant de l'âge de fer* (EN FACE) *ainsi que des plaques en hommage à Paul Kruger, qui a donné son nom au parc* (EN HAUT). *Les camps possèdent de charmants restaurants, comme celui-ci, à Letaba* (À DROITE).

SEITEN 90 UND 91 *Der Kruger Nationalpark hat nicht nur Wildbeobachtung zu bieten. Sehenswert ist auch die Stätte aus der Steinzeit im Masorini Freiluftmuseum* (GEGENÜBER) *und die Plakette zu Ehren Paul Krugers, nach dem der Park benannt ist* (OBEN). *In den Rastlagern gibt es einladende Restaurants, wie etwa dieses in Letaba* (RECHTS).

LEFT *Visitors to Skukuza go on a night drive, to see nocturnal game.*
A GAUCHE *A Skukuza les visiteurs peuvent explorer la brousse de nuit, l'idéal pour observer les animaux nocturnes.*
LINKS *Besucher unternehmen in Skukuza eine nächtliche Pirschfahrt um die nachtaktiven Tiere zu beobachten.*

BELOW *The reception area of Skukuza, the largest of the Kruger's rest camps.*
CI-DESSOUS *Le centre d'accueil de Skukuza, un des camps les plus importants du Kruger Park.*
UNTEN *Der Empfang in Skukuza, dem größten Rastlager im Kruger Nationalpark.*

ABOVE *Rondavels at Skukuza provide comfortable accommodation.*

CI-DESSUS *Les confortables logements de Skukuza.*

OBEN *Die Rundhütten in Skukuza bieten komfortable Unterkunft.*

RIGHT *A member of the Big Five, the white rhino grazes on the bushveld grass.*

À DROITE *Un des plus gros animaux sauvages, ces rhinocéros blancs paîtent dans la brousse.*

RECHTS *Ein Breitmaulnashorn – es zählt auch zu den 'Großen Fünf' – weidet in der Buschsavanne.*

PAGES 94 AND 95 *Game-viewing in Sabi Sabi, a private reserve adjacent to the Kruger* (ABOVE and TOP). *Buffalo, one of the Big Five, wallow in Kumana waterhole* (RIGHT).

PAGES 94 ET 95 *A Sabi-Sabi, une réserve privée contiguë au Kruger Park* (CI-DESSUS et EN HAUT). *Un buffle se vautre dans la vase au point d'eau de Kumana* (À DROITE).

SEITEN 94 UND 95 *Wildbeobachtung in Sabi-Sabi, einem an den Kruger Nationalpark angren-zenden privaten Wildpark* (OBEN und GANZ OBEN). *Büffel an der Wasserstelle in Kumana* (RECHTS).

FOLLOWING PAGE *A group of nesting herons silhouetted against the sunset sky.*

PAGE SUIVANTE *Un groupe de hérons se détache sur le ciel crépusculaire.*

UMSEITIG *Eine Gruppe nistender Reiher hebt sich im Dämmerlicht gegen den Himmel ab.*